MW01223995

Understanding
Business on
the Internet
in a week

*Bob Norton and
Cathy Smith*

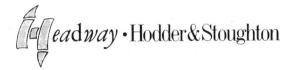

Headway · Hodder & Stoughton

British Library Cataloguing in Publication Data

A catalogue record for this title is available from the British Library

ISBN 0 340 664444

First published 1996
Impression number   10   9   8   7   6   5   4   3   2
Year   1999   1998   1997   1996

Typeset by Multiplex Techniques Ltd, St Mary Cray, Kent.
Printed in Great Britain for Hodder & Stoughton Educational,
a division of Hodder Headline Plc, 338 Euston Road, London
NW1 3BH by Redwood Books, Trowbridge, Wiltshire.

F O U N D A T I O N

The Institute of Management (IM) is at the forefront of management development and best management practice. The Institute embraces all levels of management from students to chief executives. It provides a unique portfolio of services for all managers, enabling them to develop skills and achieve management excellence.

For information on the benefits of membership, please contact:

Department HS
Institute of Management
Cottingham Road
Corby
Northants NN17 1TT

Tel: 01536 204222
Fax: 01536 201651

This series is commissioned by the Institute of Management Foundation.

CONTENTS

∎ I N T R O D U C T I O N ∎

Until the early 1990s, the Internet was known about and used mainly by academics and computer enthusiasts. There is now a much wider interest, especially from the business community, as the Internet begins to provide greater opportunities for communication, information gathering, marketing and business transactions.

Understanding Business on the Internet in a Week explains in a non-technical way why managers need to understand what the Internet is and how it could change the way they do business.

We shall look at:

Sunday	What is the Internet?
Monday	How to get access
Tuesday	Electronic mail: communications and contacts
Wednesday	Finding your way around
Thursday	Resources, uses and benefits
Friday	Marketing on the Internet
Saturday	Issues for managers

Understanding Business on the Internet in a Week offers a practical, introductory guide to a force which managers should not ignore, even if they do not use it, and on which they should make informed judgements.

What is the Internet?

There are ten questions which people ask most about the Internet. We shall deal with each of these in turn.

- What is the Internet?
- Is it the same as the Information Superhighway?
- How did the Internet start?
- Who can use it?
- How do I use it?
- How much will it cost?
- What can I do and find on the Internet?
- Can I access anybody's information anywhere?
- How do I find this information?
- What's in it for business?

What is the Internet?

Firstly, what is it not? The Internet is not a supercomputer bringing everything together in one central location. It is a worldwide network of computer networks which are connected to each other by telecommunications links. The network is made up of a variety of organisations, including government departments, universities and commercial companies which have decided to allow others to connect to their computers and share their information. It is up to each organisation how much data they make available and on what basis. In return they can use the information of other organisations. There is no owner of the Internet. The nearest thing to a governing body is a number of voluntary organisations, such as the Internet Society or the Internet Engineering Taskforce.

Is it the same as the Information Superhighway?

There are several definitions of the superhighway. To some the Internet *is* the superhighway, while to others the superhighway means better telephone and cable lines to support the Internet. To another group, the superhighway will be more than the Internet, combining various communications links including telephone, wireless and satellite. Another view is that the Internet is developing into the superhighway as it becomes an effective and secure medium for business.

How did the Internet start?

The Internet started in the 1960s when the United States military decided it needed a secure means of moving its information around the world. It set up a series of computer links (known as ARPANet) so that it did not have to rely on one route for its intelligence. This meant that if, for any reason, data was prevented from travelling in one direction it would find its way to its destination via another. It also ensured that the defence intelligence system could not easily be put out of action.

Academics soon saw the potential of the Internet for communicating with each other and exchanging research and ideas. Early computer enthusiasts also welcomed its vast possibilities for similar reasons. And there it stayed for twenty years, well known and used by these three groups – the military, the academics and the nerds or anoraks as the computer people came to be labelled. The Internet continued to be most heavily used in and influenced by the United States, although it rapidly came to be a worldwide community. In the 1980s, large companies started to use the Internet and in the 1990s, businesses of all kinds began to get connected. Networks in ninety countries now make up the Internet and this number is growing rapidly.

Who can use it?

Anybody who has a personal computer. Academics and computer enthusiasts have always been big users but there are just as many business people and ordinary consumers now. People either use the Internet to help them in their work, or at home for their hobbies, or to communicate with others, or a mix of all three.

How do I use it ?

You need a computer which can link to a network which is part of the Internet. Your organisation might be on the Internet in which case you can take advantage of a permanent connection. Most people's means of connection, however, is to subscribe to one of the commercial organisations which are willing to let you use their computer on the Internet for a fee. These firms, known as Internet Access Providers, offer access to the Internet via a telephone call, usually to a local number.

This is a very cheap means of using the Internet and has largely accounted for the phenomenal growth in interest in it. This is particularly true in North America where local calls are free in some areas. It is impossible to say how many users there are on the Internet but in 1995 it was estimated that there were over 3.5 million machines and over 35 million users. Tomorrow you will find out more about how to get access.

How much will it cost?

The costs fall into two categories: set-up and usage. You will need a personal computer with a modem. A modem is a card which sits inside the computer and turns your data input into digital signals which can be carried along normal telephone lines. These digital signals are called packets and they each contain the address label of their destination.

You will also need an arrangement with an Internet Access Provider. This company will usually charge you a one-off signing-on fee as well as a monthly usage subscription. In addition, because the Internet traffic is carried on telecommunications lines, you will have to pay telecoms connection charges, usually at the rate of a local call. Another cost of usage, that of your time, is difficult to predict because it will depend on how hooked you become: beware, the Internet is a notorious gobbler-up of time. Half an hour a day is a conservative estimate and then you have to add on the time you spend reading about it and keeping up to date with new information available and other developments.

In the past there have been few places to spend money on the Internet, because there has been no secure means of making and receiving payments. This will rapidly change, however, as the facilities become available and users begin to trust them.

You will hear more of this as we go through the week. Most computers allow you to use their information free of charge, although some are password protected, which means that you have to have prior authorisation to use the facilities.

What can I do and find on the Internet?

There are three main functions on the Internet: communication, information gathering and marketing.

Communication
The Internet is mostly used for communication and this is in the form of electronic mail. Email, as it is more popularly known, is the ability to send and receive electronic messages. Each email account on the Internet has a unique address code which allows the messages to be sent to the correct location. An email message is typed like a letter but can be received immediately like a telephone call.

Messages can be sent not only to people you know but also to people you haven't met. Special interest groups set up on the Internet allow the exchange of ideas, via email, with unknown colleagues who have similar interests. Questions can be asked of unknown experts and answers received within hours. Turn to Tuesday to find out more about email.

Information gathering
Information is available on a myriad of topics, in a variety of forms, including library holdings, product and market information, government statistics, paintings in art galleries, computer software, details of pop stars' latest albums and tours, recipes and descriptions of products and services. It

is worth remembering that this information, at the moment, largely excludes that which organisations want you to pay for and that sources can appear and disappear overnight. Turn to Thursday for more on the range of information on the Internet.

There is, however, another side to the Internet. As well as these legitimate items, anyone can also find out how to make bombs or perpetrate credit card fraud or look at pornographic material on the Internet.

Marketing
Anything from flowers to professional organisations or software is marketed on the Internet.

Some adverts are very professional, others amateurish, but all are experimental. The best provide you with useful information as they market to you. Skip to Friday for more on marketing.

Can I access anybody's information anywhere?

You can only access what others have chosen to make available. To protect data they don't want you to see, they put it behind a security wall or 'firewall', as it is known. Nothing guarantees 100% security, however, short of having two organisational networks: one on the Internet and one outside, each entirely independent of the other. See Saturday for further security issues and developments.

How do I find this information?

It can be very difficult to track what is available on the Internet and, because of the ever-increasing amount of traffic, it can be a slow process to reach the computer where the information you want is held.

There are finding tools on the Internet but the majority of these can be time-consuming to use, partly because of the vast amount of information they have to cope with. One exception is a development which has enabled the storage and retrieval of information to become easier and more palatable for computer and Internet novices. It is aptly called the World Wide Web (WWW). It allows users to move from a file of text and/or graphics to another by means of links which have been established between them. However, you still need to know the address of the computer on the WWW which holds the information you want, just as you need to know the email address of a colleague to whom you want to send a message. Turn to Wednesday for more on finding your way around.

An easy way to track information you might be interested in is to scan the daily newspapers and journals or magazines in your work or hobby-related subject area and record any addresses you think may be useful. There will certainly be some.

What's in it for business?

Commercial bodies recognised the possibilities of the Internet in the 1990s and 70 – 80% of new subscriptions now come from business. This interest was fuelled by the growth in the use of the Internet which was prompted by three main factors: the rise in the sales of personal computers, the development of the WWW and the discovery and promotion of the Internet by the media. The business community realised that here was a massive market to be tapped.

Business initially hit a problem in that the Internet community had developed its own code of ethics. In a sense it had become a network of special interest groups which operated on a mutual help and exchange basis for no commercial gain. Early attempts by commerce to sell products or services on the Internet were met by extreme anger and hostility from the Internet community. One firm which tried was hounded off the network.

The firm found, however, that along with the anger it also got many replies to its advertisement. It is getting easier all the time for commercial organisations to market on the Internet and it is becoming more acceptable as more firms attempt it. This has been made possible in large part by the advent of the WWW which has made professional, and not so professional, marketing easy and cheap to achieve. Marketing is covered in greater detail on Friday, and Saturday will deal with related business and management issues.

Ten things you can do on the Internet

- Ask questions of unknown experts
- Email the White House
- Buy a book
- Find out about company products
- Transfer software updates
- Search the library of Congress
- Read summaries of management research reports
- Look at the Mona Lisa
- Find out the Budget details
- Follow a training course

Good and bad things about the Internet

It:

- Is democratic
- Enables cheap and efficient long-distance communication
- Is great for personal networking
- Has worldwide marketing potential
- Opens up worldwide sources of information
- Has found a focal point of access in the World Wide Web

But also it:

- Is chaotic and can be slow
- Threatens users with information overload
- Is time-consuming
- Offers few guarantees of security or confidentiality
- Carries illegal, unsuitable or trivial information
- Changes every day

Summary

Today we have looked at what the Internet is, touching on its advantages and disadvantages. There are several steps which you can take to increase your knowledge:

- Read the daily press and journals in your professional area
- Talk to colleagues and friends
- Try and see a demonstration of the Internet or get half an hour's time to experiment
- Watch out for workshops in your geographical or subject area

Tomorrow we will look at the various issues involved in getting access.

How to get access

Today we will learn more about getting the appropriate connection for access to the Internet.

There are two main ways of access: through an organisational network and a leased line (known as full access) or via a dial-up connection to an Internet Access Provider. We shall look at:

- full network access
- dial-up access
- how to choose an Internet Access Provider.

Full network access

Your organisation is only likely to have full network access if it has an Information Technology (IT) department, because a fair amount of technical work is involved in setting up and maintaining a permanent link to the Internet. This link consists of a physical cable supplied by a telecoms company, such as British Telecom (BT), and a box called a router (defined in the resource requirements list below). Your connection, which will be open all the time, is likely to be to one of the backbone networks, such as Super Janet in the United Kingdom, Ebone in Europe or the American National Science Foundation's NSFNet in the United States. Most of these networks have been publicly funded but there are some commercial ventures.

Your first step, therefore, is to check with the IT department to see if it maintains a full-time link. If it does, ask if you can take advantage of it. Find out if there is any training available for new Internet users and, if not, talk to colleagues who have learnt to use the Internet and see if they are willing to pass on the benefit of their experience.

Benefits of full access
These are some of the features which a computer network with full access to the Internet has that an individual personal computer with dial-up access does not:

- its own name, usually the name of the organisation to which it belongs
- a much faster capability of sending and receiving information
- superior electronic mail capability.

Resource requirements
If your organisation does not have full access, consider the costs carefully before you recommend this option. You will need:

- a computer (or server as it is usually termed). It should be quite a powerful machine to handle incoming and outgoing traffic
- a router, which allows data signals from your network to be sent to other networks. Depending on the amount of traffic, an organisation may have more than one router. Internet Access Providers, for example, have several
- a firewall, which is a computer that sits between the Internet and your computer network acting as a device to keep intruders at bay

- a dedicated, leased line from your network to another network on the Internet, which will entail an installation and annual rental fee of significant proportions. It can be supplied directly by all the main telecoms companies, such as BT, Mercury, or Energis, or by the cable operators, or installed by an Internet Access Provider. You will need to decide on the bandwidth you want. (Bandwidth dictates the speed at which data can be carried on the line. A useful analogy is the varying speeds at which water can move, depending on the width of the pipe.) A fairly basic line (64kbps) will cost in the region of £10,000 per annum
- staff to set up and maintain your link.

Of course, you may already have the equipment and staff available if they are employed for other functions; if so these costs will be greatly reduced or more easily absorbed.

Dial-up access

Usually only large organisations have a full link to the Internet,
so most people access it via what is called a dial-up connection
from their personal computer (PC) to a commercial Internet
Access Provider. This is not a permanent connection, as with
full access, but is only active when you dial-up (as in making
an ordinary telephone call) to the provider's host computer.

Equipment checklist for dial-up access
You will need:

- a personal computer. It is difficult to outline a
  specification for a suitable state-of-the-art PC for
  Internet access when technological progress is so
  rapid. At the time of writing, however, a 486 SX 33
  megahertz is adequate. A 386 will work, but will be
  slow. It is advisable to have an expandable memory
  capacity which will enhance your capability to
  transfer and download files
- a telephone line. It doesn't matter if you use a direct
  line or have to dial out via a switchboard. It is
  important, however, to have a dedicated socket
  otherwise you are forever having to change the plug,
  depending on whether you want to use the modem or
  the telephone
- A modem. If you are buying a new PC, have the
  modem built in as part of the package. The speed of
  data transmission down the telephone lines will
  depend on the speed of the modem you use. A V32
  bis modem sending and receiving data at 14400 bits
  per second is suitable for Internet use, but 19200/
  19200 is a faster option and 28800/28800 is
  expected to become the standard. Do check that the
  modem you want to use is capable of connecting to
  your chosen Internet Access Provider

- internet access software. This has all the functionality needed to carry out tasks on the Internet, such as an email package and a browser for the WWW. Some providers send you the software on disk through the post. Others ask you to connect to their computer to copy the Internet access software to your PC. This entails you already having a piece of communications software which you need only use once and also carrying out a software transfer task (which is not straightforward for the novice)
- an account with an Internet Access Provider. Companies offering Internet access have mushroomed and offer varying rates and services. Later today we look at various aspects to consider when choosing a provider. Telephone numbers of some of the UK providers are given at the end of this chapter.

Access problems

Dial-up access is very cheap (see the following section on costs) but is subject to the vagaries of what is happening on the data lines or on the remote host computer which allows you Internet access. It is important to recognise that things can and will go wrong from time to time. Some of the disadvantages are summarised below:

- as the connection isn't permanent, electronic mail which is sent to you doesn't come straight to your computer. You have to dial-up and collect it from the provider
- access can be slow (but is improved with faster modem speeds)

- the host computer is sometimes unavailable because of maintenance or other difficulties
- providers can get overloaded because of the sheer number of users, particularly first thing in the morning. The data lines can get very busy in the afternoon when North America is awake.

Costs

There are two kinds of charges you pay for a dial-up connection:

- internet Access Provider fees. These usually include a one-off signing-on fee plus either a flat rate fee for unlimited monthly usage or a fee for each time you access the Internet. Your choice will depend on how much you think you will use the service. When you join up it is probably worth going

for a provider which offers unlimited usage under a
flat rate fee because it is staggering how quickly the
time passes while you are learning and
experimenting. £200 per annum is a standard
charge at 1995/6 prices

- telecoms charges. You will also incur these charges
as you are using the telephone lines to reach the
provider. They can soon mount up, so in order to
reduce them, the Internet providers offer contact
telephone numbers or, in Internet parlance, 'Points of
Presence' (PoPs) around the country. The idea is
that any user should only need to contact a local
number and pay a local call rate. Unfortunately, there
are a limited number of PoPs and unless you live near
one you will have to pay a long distance call.

How to choose an Internet Access Provider

Providers quickly earn a reputation for what they offer.
Consider the factors listed below and ask other users what
their experience of various providers has been.

1.   *Try out the service*
Can you try the service before you buy it? This might be
possible at an exhibition (there is a large Internet exhibition
held in London every Spring) or at a seminar (there are
more and more hands-on training workshops available).
There are now several Cybercafés around the UK where you
can buy a cappuccino and have half an hour, or an hour's
trial on the Internet very cheaply. Look out for offers where
you can explore the Internet free of charge for a period.

2.   *Check the fee rates*

Find out the various fee structures, how much it costs for
unlimited usage and how much cheaper, or more expensive,
it might be if you pay as you use. Be wary of special deals,
such as the waiving of the signing-on fee, which are
sometimes used to promote a particular supplier. The real
payment is in the usage and the key issue is deciding
whether to connect on a flat rate or pay-as-you-go basis.

3.   *Assess the ease of use of the software and what it contains*

Find out how easy it is to install the software: do you have
to transfer it to your computer down the telephone lines or
are you sent the software on disk? Will you be able to install
it yourself or will you require assistance from a friend or
colleague or even from a specialist?

Ask what the interface is like and how easy it is to use, for
example if it is DOS or Windows based. Check that a browser
to enable you to use the WWW is supplied in the software.
Find out if subscribers receive software updates or at least if
they are told which version of the software the provider is
currently supporting and where and how to get hold of it. See
Wednesday for more on software file transfer.

4.   *Ensure that adequate support is available*

Does the provider have a help desk number? If so, how
easy is it to get through to? How helpful and friendly are the
staff? Some providers seem to assume that users are already
skilled computer users.

Most providers include help files in the software but these
can be unintelligible to the novice or do not seem to contain
the information you need.

5. Establish the number of PoPs available

Ask if the supplier only has one London access point or
several around the country. What are their plans for
opening more PoPs and where will they be? This is
important because it means the difference between a local
and a long-distance call and a correspondingly low or high
telephone bill. Check also the effectiveness of the provider's
connection to the Internet: is it a direct or indirect link? Is
the company reselling another provider's services?

6. Investigate the provider's reputation

Try and find out any background information on the
providers, for example, has there been any transfer of
personnel around the providers or do any of them have
powerful partnerships with other companies to help them
provide the service?

Internet Access Providers
These are the names and telephone numbers of some of the
many companies offering Internet access in the United
Kingdom:

BTNet:	0345 585110
Cityscape:	01223 566950
Cix:	01492 641961
Demon:	0181 371 1234
Easynet:	0171 209 0990
EUNet:	01227 266466
Pipex:	01223 250120

Microsoft's Windows95, which is likely to have a huge effect
on the personal computer market, will include an
application called Microsoft Network. This will give users
access to email but, at the time of writing, it is unclear what
the level of access to the Internet as a whole will be, on what
basis and how much it will cost.

Training providers
Many organisations offer regular or one-off Internet training
courses. Find out what is available in your geographical
area by consulting the local press, colleges, TEC or Chamber
of Commerce. Check what is offered in your subject area by
monitoring the professional journals.

Summary

Today we have looked at the equipment you will need for
full and dial-up access and advised you to take a little time
in choosing an Internet Access Provider, asking the views of
existing users if possible. Tomorrow we will look at sending
and receiving electronic mail, the first steps most people
take on the Internet.

Electronic mail: communications and contacts

Electronic mail is the most widely used function on the Internet. Best estimates put email use at 85% of all Internet traffic. Companies offering email facilities have been around for several years but the interest in and use of email has really grown because the Internet has made it much cheaper to use and because high-speed, efficient and low-cost modems, which are necessary to relay it, have become available. Today we look at:

- What is electronic mail?
- Email addresses
- Netiquette
- Newsgroups and discussion lists
- Managers' thoughts on email
- Advantages and disadvantages of email.

What is electronic mail?

Electronic mail, or email as it is more commonly known, is an electronic cross between letters, telephone calls and faxes.

- Like a letter an email message has to be written down but it can be informal like a telephone call
- Like a telephone call it is sent along the telephone lines but is split into 'packets' which may travel by a variety of routes and is then put together again at its destination

- Like a fax, but unlike a telephone call, it can be sent at a time convenient to the sender and read at a time convenient to the recipient. This is particularly useful where the correspondents are in different time zones or where it avoids the recipient being interrupted by the message, in the case of a sales person with a customer, for example
- Like a telephone call it is a very immediate form of communication but with the mixed blessing that your thoughts are in writing
- Unlike a telephone call it does not allow simultaneous two-way communication, although messages can bounce forwards and backwards very quickly, giving a conversation of sorts
- Like a fax or letter it can handle not only text but also graphics
- Like a fax, messages can be relayed from one to one, or one to many, with only one copy of the original document

- Like a letter, fax or telephone call you need to know the address of the person to whom you are sending a message. However, it is also possible to send messages to a group of people where you know their collective address but not their individual ones. This latter facility, where people with the same interests set up what are called newsgroups or discussion lists, gives email users great power, permitting them to exchange information and opinions with people they have never met
- Email users do not have to be at home or at their desk to read their messages; all they need to do is to dial into their Internet Access Provider. An email address means you are not tied to a place to access it, like a traditional postal address

Users in organisations which have the advantage of full Internet access have email sent straight to their PC or terminal so that they are alerted to new messages when they log in or as they are working. They can also send messages as soon as they are written. Dial-up users experience a delay as they must connect to their Internet Access Provider to collect and receive their email. The most economical way to use email for a dial-up Internet user is to read and write messages off-line (i.e. when you are not connected to the Internet Access Provider) and only go on-line (connect) when you want to collect or send messages.

Email addresses

Each person using email on the Internet has a unique address which has several parts to it. For example, *bloggs_j@easynet.co.uk*

is made up in the following way:

bloggs_j – the computer username of the user

@ – 'is found at'

easynet – the name of the host computer which is on the Internet

co – the type of organisation which owns the host computer, in this case a company, but there are also other codes, such as *ac* for academic organisations, *org* for non-profit making organisations and *gov* for government departments and agencies. (These codes may vary from country to country. For example, in the United States, *ac* is replaced by *edu*)

uk – the country code. All countries have a code except the USA where the Internet started.

Other examples of addresses include:

president@whitehouse.gov

santa@north.pole.org

institute@easynet.co.uk

Don't be surprised if you sometimes come across addresses that look different. These will be based at email services which used to be outside the Internet. For example, 70006.101@compuserve.com, is the customer service address for CompuServe which has long provided business and private individuals with access to email and database, and latterly, Internet facilities.

Finding addresses

There are email address directories available, but with such rapid growth in email usage, their coverage can only be patchy at best. The best option is to build up your own directory over time by collecting those addressses which you use regularly, or those which may be useful at some stage. These can be found on email you receive, for example, or on business cards, in the press and on the radio and television. Telephoning or faxing people for their email address is accepted practice. Remember that everyone else is in the same boat so help them by publicising your own address.

Netiquette

As we have mentioned, email is a very immediate form of communication which allows you to write in haste and regret at your leisure. To try and mitigate this and to overcome the limitations of a medium which does not allow for normal visual and audio reactions, a system of Internet etiquette, or 'netiquette' as it has been dubbed, has evolved. Use of capital letters denotes SHOUTING or ANGER. A list of characters known as 'smileys' are used to give extra meaning to words, for example

:-) means that the writer is happy
;-) is a wink and a smile.

Abbreviations are also popular, for example:

AISI	As I see it
BTW	By the way
HTH	Hope this helps
IMHO	In my humble opinion
FAQ	Frequently asked/answered question
FYI	For your information.

Newsgroups and discussion lists

Suppose you would like to correspond with others who share your leisure and work interests but you are not sure where to find them. Email allows you to join newsgroups or discussion lists where like-minded people swap news, gossip, discuss new developments, ask each other questions and send information and advice. This is done by sending a message to the group's email address and this gets passed on to everyone else in the group and you get everyone else's messages in return. You can be a part of a group for as short or as long a time as you like. You can be entirely passive and just read the messages which come in or take an active part by forwarding messages.

Newsgroups
A listing of the newsgroups available appears in most providers' software and it is fairly straightforward to select those that you wish to take part in. Beware though, once you join a group you can receive tens or hundreds of messages a day so don't be too enthusiastic in joining too many at first. Depending on the software you use, either all messages will be downloaded from the Internet Access Provider's computer each time you log in or you can run through the list of what is available at that time and choose to download only those which you wish to read in detail.

Examples of newsgroups
The following give you a flavour of the newsgroups available (alt. just means 'alternative'; misc. stands for miscellaneous; and rec. is short for 'recreation'):

```
alt.fan.madonna
alt.education.research
alt.business.seminars
alt.management.tech-support
alt.alien.research
misc.business.consulting
misc.business.facilitators
rec.autos.sport.f1
rec.music.classical
```

Discussion lists

Discussion lists work in a slightly different way and tend to be more specialised and for a smaller group of people. They are often moderated which means that they are overseen by one or more people who control what goes through to the list. This is a way, for example, of filtering out unwelcome adverts from individuals and companies wishing to sell their products or services. On occasions when adverts do get through to a list, it is common for the originators to be 'flamed', that is receive a reply containing a strong opinion that the message is unwelcome. When tens and hundreds of people do this the offender's computer can grind to a halt.

Discussion lists are a good forum for clubs, groups and committees to keep in touch, receive minutes of meetings and exchange information.

Examples of discussion lists

bpr	Business process reengineering
hrnet	Human resources network
learning-org	Learning organisation
leadrshp	Leaders and leadership
management-research	Management research
trdev-l	Training and development
telework	Teleworking

The authoritative guide to discussion lists is *The Directory of Scholarly Electronic Conferences* by Diane Kovacs. This is available from the United States Association of Research Libraries or via the Internet in various forms.

Managers' thoughts on email

'My initial email activity has been to correspond with friends and ex-colleagues who are not within easy reach.'

'Here everybody uses email as much as possible, thus reducing the amount of paper used. It is a very efficient way of checking what is going on and you do not risk losing an important note or report. You receive the information very fast and can act very fast too. It is also cheaper than using the phone. It's fun just to be able to communicate so easily with all sorts of people.'

'Whenever I have placed a request for help on one of the newsgroups I have usually had the correct answer within twenty-four hours.'

'Whilst communicating around the newsgroups I have built up a friendship with people around the world.'

'We use email a lot; I receive forty-plus messages daily, from countries such as the USA, Australia and Germany and sometimes from Turkey and Russia.'

'I set up as a consultant last year. My email address allows me to talk to my clients (many large companies now have email). I also subscribe to a number of newsgroups which keep me appraised of professional developments as well as providing a network of contacts.'

'I am using email to swap data between the various companies in our group. We are an international company. Using a mail box means we are not tied to any routine or physical presence.'

'I joined primarily to be able to send electronic mail to my daughter at university.'

Advantages and disadvantages of email

Advantages
- Delivery is faster than traditional mail or 'snail mail' as email users like to call it
- It overcomes time zone differences as the recipient does not have to be available to receive it
- One-to-many correspondence is simple
- An email address is portable
- It enables you to exchange information with people previously unknown to you
- As the information is carried in electronic form and can easily be reused
- The cost is not dependent on the distance the message has to travel
- It is much cheaper than fax or telephone
- Replying to messages is straightforward because the reply facility includes the originator's address

Disadvantages
- It is not very secure; anyone can intercept and read your email if they really want to
- Devotees can become over-exuberant in its use and bombard you regularly, some with long, rambling messages

THANK YOU FOR YOUR 17th MESSAGE THIS MORNING...

- Sometimes the apparent immediacy of email, like fax, can panic you into thinking that you need to respond straight away. Unlike a letter, the immediacy can take over
- It can be used inappropriately, for example, a long document, unless urgent, is better posted in the traditional way thereby saving the recipient's time and paper in printing it out
- You can become a postbox for other people who do not have an email account but have friends and contacts who do
- It encourages off-the-cuff replies which you may regret later
- Printouts of email can look rather untidy; this is most likely to occur when you are sending to a mail system which is different from the one you use

Summary

Today we have looked at how email works, what it is used for and its advantages and disadvantages. As well as communication, it is a way of finding information. Other ways of finding information on the Internet will be considered tomorrow.

Finding your way around

There is so much information available on the Internet that it is easy to flounder about and get confused.

Today we highlight the main functions available, other than email, and give some pointers on how you can find your way around. We shall look at:

- Searching databases (Telnet)
- Transferring files from one computer to another (FTP)
- Using the World Wide Web
- Search tools
- A map of the Internet

We shall particularly concentrate on the World Wide Web.
Apart from email, this is the part of the Internet which is
easiest to use and is the most useful for business.

Searching databases (Telnet)

The Internet gives you the opportunity to search databases,
such as library catalogues, previously unavailable except to
staff of the host organisation. The ability to do this is
offered by the Telnet protocol. This allows you to enter the
address of the computer you want to visit and log in as an
anonymous user. Some computers are password protected
which means that you need to register with the organisation
beforehand. Telnet merely takes you to the host computer;
once there, you are inside the environment of the host
computer and therefore subject to its own search language.
The other requirement is that you will usually be asked to
configure your PC to emulate the type of terminal
connection suitable for the remote computer.

Transferring files from one computer to another (FTP)

Thousands of computers on the Internet have files which are
freely available to the public.

These range from computer programs to the text of Alice in
Wonderland.

If you wish to retrieve a file, you need to use a file transfer protocol (usually referred to as FTP) which ensures that data stored on one computer can be transmitted to another.

FTP is probably the most difficult function to master on the Internet, although if your Internet Access Provider has given you menu-based software, then it becomes easier. In essence, you need to know the address of the computer which holds the file you require, log in using 'anonymous' as your username and your email address as your password, and then transfer the file. (To help you identify the files you may find of interest, see the Search tools below.)

There are some major FTP sites around the world: the main one in the UK is at Imperial College, London *(ftp src.doc.ic. ac.uk)*.

Using the World Wide Web (WWW)

The Web has done much to reduce the mystery of the
Internet and transform it into a useable resource. It is a
programme which cross references, links and retrieves data
from computers around the world using what is called a
hypertext system. This allows you to move from one
document to another using a mouse to click on highlighted
terms or graphics. The moves are seamless, enabling you
to find information in all forms: graphics, video and sound
as well as text. The information you will find on the WWW
is extraordinarily diverse as anyone with a computer,
modem and a little expertise can set up a Web page. You
can see the jokes and family snapshots of Joe Bloggs side by
side with data from the CIA and NASA.

All documents on the WWW have a unique address, known
as a Uniform Resource Locator (URL), which has several
parts to it. For example, Virgin Atlantic's address is: http://
www.demon.co.uk/atlantic and is made up as follows:

http:// – hypertext transfer protocol
www.demon.co.uk – usually the name of the server
   that belongs to the organisation
atlantic – the directory in which the information is held

In some cases a file name may be specified. In that case a
slash(/) would be used to separate the file name from the
directory name.

Other protocols can also be used on the Web such as *ftp://* and *telnet://*.

To use the WWW you need a browser. A browser views documents by talking over the Internet to the computers where the information is held. You can telnet to a remote computer which holds a browser, but it is highly preferable to have one on your own PC. There are a number of browsers, but two have emerged as market leaders. One is called Mosaic, the other Netscape. Both are subject to rapid upgrading and can be downloaded from sites on the Internet by FTP, usually free of charge if used for non-commercial activities. Otherwise, a licence fee must be paid to the browser's owners. More of the WWW on Thursday and Friday.

Search tools

A major headache is finding out what information is available and where it is located. The tools listed below are, we suggest, last resorts as they are not straightforward to use and will turn up many sources of information. A search on general management will yield thousands of potential places to visit, for example. Other more comfortable ways of identifying sources of information include the press, the professional journals in your subject area and recommendations from friends and colleagues. Do bear in mind, however, that there is constant change on the Internet. Sites can appear overnight and disappear just as quickly.

Archie

The search system for FTP files is called Archie. It was constructed at McGill University in Montreal. There are numerous Archie servers available around the world, each containing more or less the same information. To reach one of these you need to perform a telnet operation. Once there, you can scan indexes containing information on all anonymous FTP sites on the Internet. The indexes are updated regularly.

Gopher

Another way of identifying which FTP files and remote databases are available is by using a tool called Gopher, devised at the University of Minnesota. Gopher is variously stated to mean a little furry animal that burrows for things, or 'go for'.

A Gopher is a computer program which organises files in a standard menu format in order to browse the contents.

Menus lead to other menus and so on. Thousands of computers are set up as Gophers, and also provide automatic access to other Gophers. There is also a system called Veronica, found within many Gopher menus, which searches across hundreds of Gopher servers. If you want to try using Gopher, telnet to a computer which holds this facility.

Web crawlers

The Gopher system has ceded primacy of place to the World Wide Web not only because menu-based systems are being replaced by graphical interfaces but also because the Web covers so much more (the WWW will take you to gopher servers if a link has been set up, for example). However, the WWW still has a need for search tools of its own.

With thousands of organisations putting up information on the WWW, a printed directory would be obsolete long before you flicked it open. Instead you can use a 'crawler', also called a 'robot' or 'spider'. A crawler is an indexing and location device for information sitting on other computers. It is a massive search and find program resident at various major Internet sites that regularly scours other sites for information. There are a number of crawlers available and they vary in the type of search they offer, ease of use and the speed and efficiency of their retrieval. Try the same search on one or two of them as the relevance of a site may be increased if a number of services have indexed it. Here are several which have begun to emerge as useful finding tools.

- WebCrawler, which was developed at the University of Washington, brings hundreds of thousands of documents into its net by tracking occurences of terms from one document to another and one computer to another. The WebCrawler is updated daily and will provide a list of search results in descending order of their relevance. *http://webcrawler.com*
- Lycos, which was developed at the Carnegie Mellon University, provides an index to some 4,000,000 Web pages. Lycos allows you to refine your search and limit the number of results you get, thus speeding up the process. *http://lycos.cs.cmu.edu*
- Einet's Galaxy can search across links established by the WWW and gopher computers. It also has its own extensive A-Z subject list. Einet's Galaxy also indicates the size of the document retrieved; like a book you can see how long it is before deciding to read it. *http://galaxy.einet.net/galaxy/Business-and-Commerce.html*
- The WorldWideWebWorm won an award in 1994 for its search and retrieval capability. *http://www.netgen.com/cgi/wandex*
- Yahoo stands for Yet Another Hierarchical Organized Oracle. It has a business page which provides links to 11,000 sites via a series of headings. *http://www.yahoo.com/business*
- AliWeb stands for Archie Like Indexing of the Web. This is a public service that requests people to send them details of their web pages, such as subject coverage and address details. *http://web.nexor.co.uk/public/aliweb*

Sorting the Information These crawler sites will still provide information on a staggering scale. Once you have retrieved 400 or even forty items of interest, how do you tackle them? One answer lies in relevance ranking, or sorting the items in terms of their relevance to your original request. Basically, you find one or two documents out of the mass which seem most appropriate to your needs, click on them with your mouse button, and then the rest are automatically sorted in terms of relevance. Keep an eye open for the possibility of relevance ranking; it can save a lot of time. Some sites, for example Lycos and WebCrawler, have this capability installed.

Another method of selection, evaluation and elimination is to go for those sites which have already carried out some initial selection process. They enable you to scan for your interests from a menu of sources they have constructed. For example, the University of Nijenrode in the Netherlands has compiled a useful and easy-to-use resource list of freely available business information sources (*http://www.nijenrode. nl/nbr*). This has a number of major business headings, such as Accounting and Taxation; Finance and Banking; Marketing; Entrepreneurship; and International Business.

Map of the Internet

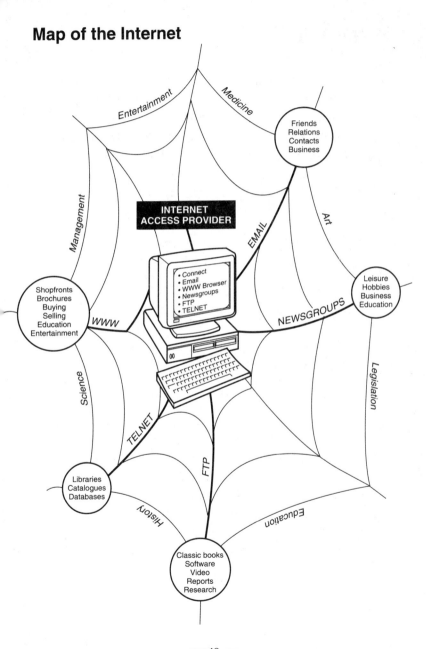

Summary

- There is an enormous amount of information available and therefore there is a need to adopt some ruthless selection and elimination procedures
- There is constant change on the Internet: sites appear and disappear rapidly

- Transmission speeds can be slow, particularly in the afternoons when both Europe and America are using the Internet. You need patience, especially when using the WWW, as the painting of graphics is particularly affected. Small print on some sites may indicate that you can dispense with graphics and opt for text only. This will lose some of the visual impact but will speed up the process, especially if you are connected via a modem
- Search tools are poor but improving

- Finding your way around is easier if you have a menu-based front end which automates some of the work involved in logging on to remote computers and transferring files
- By the Internet's very nature you are visiting other organisation's computers as you search for information. Bear in mind that you are a guest on their system and that you should therefore treat their site courteously. Try to avoid times when they are likely to be busy and understand if they refuse access. Don't spend too long on any one site.

Tomorrow we will look at the type of information you can find on the Internet, how managers are using it and what benefits they derive.

Resources, uses and benefits

Now that we know how to get there and what's out there, what use are people making of the Internet? More importantly what benefits are they deriving? Today we shall look at:

- The resources that the Internet offers
- Ways of putting the Internet to use
- Case studies of managers' experiences

The resources that the Internet offers

There is quite simply a staggering amount of information which can only be measured in thousands of terabytes or millions of pages. It is a sobering thought that since the 1970s the world's output of information has grown exponentially, although it was as far back as 1830 that a scientist found he could no longer cope with all the new information relevant to his field. Most, if not all, of the information produced in recent years is in electronic form, and a large proportion of it is American in origin.

Another sobering thought is the democratic and anarchic character of the Internet where everyone's voice can be heard and everyone can be a publisher. Until recently the ethos of the Internet has been the free dissemination of thoughts and ideas as opposed to the evaluation and control usually found in commercially valuable or exploitable information.

That doesn't mean to say that the Internet can be easily ignored although it is often dismissed as a forum for the exchange of recipes and gardening tips.

There are a number of factors mitigating against rejection of all information sources on the Internet. The first and foremost is that it caters for a wide variety of personal, leisure and non-business activities. It is important to remember that the Internet widens the opportunity for pursuing these interests. Other reasons for taking the Internet seriously include a change in its culture as business and commercial interests become more involved, and the increase in the number of directional and selection tools.

These are a few examples of information sites that you can find on the Internet. Remember that they can change and disappear very rapidly!

Commercial organisations
Many corporate giants now offer value-added services to customers on the Internet, but it is not the exclusive domain of big business. It is as easy for small and medium-sized businesses to set up on the WWW; many of these have led the way and the giants have followed. Here are examples of just a few of the thousands of commercial organisations offering information and services:

Ernst and Young (accountancy publications) *http:// www.ernsty.co.uk/ernsty*

Microsoft Corporation *http://www.microsoft.com*

J Sainsbury (company activities and initiatives; customer services including recipes and a direct wine purchasing service) *http://www.j-sainsbury.co.uk*

Virgin Atlantic (flight schedules, fare options and frequent flyer programmes) *http://www.demon.co.uk/atlantic*

Educational organisations
The MBA Page (prepared by the Fisher College of Business at Ohio State University to offer help and advice to MBA students) *http://www.cob.ohio-state.edu/dept/fin/ mba.htm*

Open University *http://www.open.ac.uk/*

Southampton Institute MBA *http://www.cecomm.co.uk*

Virtual Online University *http://www.iac.net/~billp/*

Government bodies
NASA (space images) *http://images.jsc.nasa.gov/html/home.htm*

STAT-USA (from the US Department of Commerce; acts as an outlet for the US government's business, trade and economic information) *http://www.stat-usa.gov/*

Department of Trade and Industry *http://www.dti.gov.uk*

CCTA government information service *http://www.open.gov.uk*

UK government press releases (including those from the Census Office, Trade and Industry, the Home Office, Transport, Environment, Social Security and the Revenue) *http://www.coi.gov.uk/coi/depts/deptlist.html*

UK government Treasury information *http://www.hm-treasury.gov.uk*

Management
The Management Archive (forum for management ideas and information. Provides access to contributed working papers and preprints in the management and organisational sciences, course syllabi and teaching materials, conference announcements and archives of the Academy of Management.) *gopher://ursus.jun.alaska.edu:70*

Soundview Executive Book Summaries (includes abbreviated versions of the management book reviews that are published in hard copy. Other services include business questions and answers and management ideas of the week) *http:// www.summary.com*

Technology and Operations Management (this is a group at the Harvard Business School which includes links to working papers and the TQM group's quarterly electronic newsletter) *http://rigel.hbs.harvard.edu*

Uncover (on-line table of contents index and article delivery service for approximately 17,000 magazines and journals) *http:// www.carl.org/uncover/unchome.html*

The Press
The Economist *http://www.economist.com*

The Daily Telegraph *http://www.telegraph.co.uk* (a freely available password is needed to access this site)

Dow Jones News Service *http://www.dowjones.com*

Electronic Newsstand *http://www.enews.com:2102/enews.html*

The Financial Times *http://www.ft.com*

Harvard Business Review (abstracts of articles in current issue) *http://deadendx.harvard.edu/web/hbsshow/hbr/current/ HBR.html*

Recreation
List of football club servers *http:// www.atm.ch.cam.ac.uk/
sports/webs.html*

Movie Browser *http://www.cm.cf.ac.uk/movies/moviequery.html*

Rolling Stones *http://www.stones.com*

General interest
BBC *http://www.bbcnc.org.uk/*

UK weather (Met office forecasts) *http://www.elec.qmw.ac.uk/
~markj/paraglide/uk_weather.html*

Travel advice notices from the Foreign and Commonwealth
Office *http://www.fco.gov.uk/reference/travel_advice/
advice.html*

London (restaurants and pubs) *http://www.cs.ucl.ac.uk/misc/
uk/london.html*

Paris Pages (What's new) *http://www.paris.org/whatsnew.html*

About New York City *http://www.gc.cuny.edu/other/
AboutNYC.html*

The Millennium *http://www.milfac.co.uk/*

The official list of British Web pages *http://src.doc.ic.ac.uk/all-
uk.html*

Ways of putting the Internet to use

If 85% of all Internet traffic is email, what is the other 15%
used for? At the moment, research on managers' use of the
Internet is thin on the ground, partly because it is such a

new medium for most. A recent survey of business use of the Internet found, however, that 72% of the respondents felt that the Internet had the potential to become a key source of business information and 27% of users said it was currently contributing to their business. On the other hand, 37% were dissatified with it and 48% believed it had been overhyped. An informal survey of members of the Institute of Management found that while some claimed to have 'no time for surfin', others are, albeit haltingly, beginning to find it useful.

- Academics are using the Internet as a teaching medium with online conferencing, and as an information resource. They often create local discussion lists for students to use.
- Publishers and authors are using email to transmit copy for the collation of magazines, to perform on-line editing and to cut down production time.

- Small business and consultants are using appropriate newsgroups for kick-starting new projects by asking for help, advice or sources of information. Others trawl the 'wider' Internet for data sources and contact points listed in the web-crawlers we saw yesterday.
- Organisations with international links use the Internet for cheap communications, staying in touch, news gathering on industries and competitors and seeking out collaborators.
- Supermarkets are offering on-line ordering of groceries, and pizza houses allow you to create and order your own pizza over the Internet.

- Many larger organisations are using the Internet to support telecommuting and working from home. In some cases, virtual businesses have been created where people may only meet face-to-face occasionally.

- Transportation and tourism companies are using it for advance warning of traffic news, weather conditions and travel arrangements.
- Museums are using the Internet to advertise exhibits and events by putting up full-colour images which users can download to their own PC.
- Shopping malls have sprung up where flowers, books and goods of all sorts are sold.
- One highly creative use is that of a bakery using the Internet to connect to weather forecasting services to determine what kind of produce to make available, rain or shine.

Case studies of managers' experiences

The consultant

'I was able to use the Internet to access the virus name database of my software supplier on a Sunday afternoon, get an answer in a few minutes and reassure a worried client that she almost certainly did not have a virus on her computer. I had the option to download the latest anti-virus package if needed. I have obtained up-to-date printer drivers from both Microsoft and Hewlett Packard. I recently ordered various free catalogues from HMSO, browsing their database at leisure on a Sunday. I have discovered a lot of health-related information in the UK and elsewhere which will be useful. I accessed the US Department of Health to try to get some information on toxic chemicals and found a lot of data which will be valuable to a client in the future. The most useful service any company can provide via the

Internet in the first instance is to enable people to download their product data sheets. Clients nearly always want those yesterday.'

The management academic
'I'm a full-time management academic, but a part-time consultant and trainer also. I have in excess of forty associates and we use the Internet as our prime means of communication. As I largely work from home, email is a major means of communication with work colleagues and I have a growing number of contacts with students and friends outside the working environment. I also use the Internet as a teaching medium. We have a number of computer conferences and a course taught on- and off-line. Finally, the Internet provides a wider variety of research sources than I could previously access and this is a major saving of time and energy.'

The director and publisher
'I am the director of a games company as well as a management consultant. The magazine published by the company every month is built almost entirely of submissions transmitted across the Internet. Much of the news which we publish is gleaned from the Web and from newsgroups. These also give me access to a wide repository of expertise that is provided freely and enthusiastically.'

The market researcher

'The opportunity of carrying out market research on the Internet is exciting and frustrating. I had an assignment on the take-up of cable television and would have loved to have carried out a survey on the Internet. At the moment I'm writing a market research report on the catering industry and there appears to be no hard information about independent, outside caterers. I've also had an abortive attempt to shop on the Internet. The idea was good as my sister lives in New York and I thought I could order a present from a New York store via the Internet. One success though! A friend was going off to Moscow and I was able to use the weather information to get the Moscow report.'

The writer

'I have used the WWW to give me background knowledge of the cities my film star subjects lived in or visited during their lifetimes. For instance, one of my subjects lived for a time in West Hollywood and going into the West Hollywood Web page gave me information on the culture of the area as well as on the population of the city. The Internet also helped me build contacts in Los Angeles, where I travelled recently to carry out some research on my latest subject. I mailed a message to one of the newsgroups, asking for information about LA. I was contacted by an LA resident who emailed me advice and tips on how to get the best out of my visit.'

The software engineer

'We use the newsgroups to read about past experiences of other people with particular products. For example, when we needed to upgrade a PC, browsing the relevant newsgroups indicated what hardware was "flavour of the month". Practically all the computer products (hardware and software) we now purchase are supported on Web pages. This makes it easy to contact the manufacturer when problems occur and the ability to download upgrades ensures that we are always operating our equipment at optimum levels. Finally, we develop software using the compiler supplied by Borland. Recently, they had a developers' conference in the United States and within a couple of days the transcripts of the presentations were available from their Web site which gave us information on the strategic goals of the Borland compiler group.'

Summary

Today we have looked at the information available through the Internet and at the ways in which some managers are using it. Tomorrow we will look at how companies are using the Internet to market themselves and offer some advice on putting up information on your own organisation.

Marketing on the Internet

The Internet is a new marketing medium, full of promise but to be treated with some caution. It is wise to watch and learn from the experience and mistakes of others and to observe the ground rules which are emerging. Today we will tackle marketing on the Internet, mainly by concentrating on the World Wide Web. Marketing via Newsgroups can be done, but is still frowned on and so must be used with restraint. We ask:

- What have others done?
- Who's out there?
- What's different about it?
- Where do you start?
- What are the cost factors?
- What kind of marketing strategies can be used?
- What are the key criteria for success?

What have others done?

Early companies looking to market on the Internet found their heads turned by the worldwide market and barraged the newsgroups *en masse* with advertisements. But the tactic backfired. They were swamped with so many angry calls and complaints (or 'flames' as they are called by Internet users) that their computers were jammed and they promised not to do it again.

They were unfortunate in being the first to challenge the non-commercial ethos of the Internet and they failed to pay attention to targeting their adverts to those most likely to be interested.

However, these organisations were successful in that:

a) they got their message through
b) it was a very low-cost exercise compared to normal advertising
c) they did get replies.

Other organisations learnt the lessons of this experience and targeted a handful of newsgroups which might be especially interested in their product or service. Although they still got some flak, they began to benefit from the changing culture of the Internet and found it more receptive to marketing. They were less aggressive, more focused in their approach, ready and willing to take their time, and learn. And they have begun to pick up business.

The shift in stance towards marketing has taken place since the advent of the WWW. This has made it easy for firms to write advertisements and allowed consumers to come to the advertising site rather than being bombarded with what they regard as junk mail.

One company launched a new product exclusively by means of the WWW. Within a couple of days, they received enquiries from all over the world, magazines called to run features on it, technical reviewers asked for a sample, and the company was asked to present their new product at an international conference.

Who's out there?

If the essence of marketing and mailing is in targeting, how many people are there on the Internet and who are they?

Accurate figures are not knowable but recent estimates put the figure at 35 million users worldwide, increasing by a million a month. In the UK alone, it is estimated that there are about 500,000 users, a figure which is rising fast. One commentator has projected that at current rates of growth everyone on the planet will be connected by the year 2003! Not all those who use the Internet, however, are potential customers, particularly if their Internet access is work-related and focused on communication and information gathering.

The only early profile of the Internet user that has so far been established is that of the ABC1 35-year-old male, described as literate, trend-setting and libertarian, who believes in freedom of speech and the right of every group to be heard.

The Internet 'trekkie', however, is becoming a less dominant character as business takes up use of the Internet. The change has been described as a shift from 'anoraks' to 'suits'.

In reality, a mix of people use the Internet, but that excludes large sectors of the population who are either less computer-literate than others, such as the retired, or those without easy access to computers, such as the unemployed.

What's different about it?

How do you exploit the Internet as a market-place? We have identified ten ground rules.

1. Electronic consumers cannot be treated like television viewers, newspaper readers or people looking at billboards. Newsgroup messages are not delivered to a person's letter-box like postal mail. Consumers log in when they like, glance at the subject of messages, take

what they like and ignore the rest. You will not know who has read your message unless they contact you. With a WWW site, again the consumer chooses where to visit and when, and for how long. However, the WWW does enable you to monitor the visitors.

2. As the user chooses to look at the organisation's information, the necessity to make it interesting and attractive is just as important as for TV- or paper-based advertising. Just as in the real world, Internet users have many claims on their attention and are becoming increasingly sophisticated and demanding.

3. There are almost no restrictions, apart from cost, to the amount of information you can make available. This availability is for twenty-four hours a day and on Sundays. The WWW does not close.

4. Because of the Internet's potential for reaching consumers on a hitherto unknown scale, the avoidance of brash marketing expletive and unsubstantiated hype is all the more important. If you make a promise you cannot deliver, thousands of people could know about it in minutes. An upset customer will quickly pass on dissatisfaction.

5. Electronic communications are interactive: recipients have a very easy facility for rapid reply, so marketing is no longer merely one-way. The sending organisation can, within minutes of transmission, receive a message saying 'don't send again', another complaining, another suggesting improvements and another expressing an interest in buying. If they have asked a question, they will expect a quick response. In the past the advertiser has invaded the consumer's living room; now the consumer can return the compliment.

Because of this two-way communication, the potential for building relationships with consumers, wherever they may be, is vastly increased.

6. The best WWW sites are those which are interesting, hold your attention, and have more to offer than marketing hype. They are updated to keep them fresh, alive and therefore attractive for people to revisit.

7. Small companies can now hope to reach an international market-place without the infrastructure of a huge multinational organisation. The Internet enables Jones & Co. to stand side by side with the Times Top 1000 in the market-place, competing for customers.

8. Market entry can be easy and low-cost on the Internet. This increases the need for businesses to track what others are doing.

9. With a possible market stretching from Alaska to Taiwan, and Scandinavia to Australia, remember that cultural differences and sensitivities will apply.

10. Paying for products and services in a secure and confidential way will be resolved in the immediate future. Developments and experiments with electronic payments will be summarised on Saturday. In the meantime it is unreliable to send credit card numbers out into the digital networks, as there are genuine fears of interception and electronic theft. Most Internet business currently uses the traditional media to relay confidential financial information. But do watch the press for developments, as changes are coming about very quickly.

Where do you start?

Here are some guidelines on putting up pages on the World Wide Web.

1. Figure out if marketing on the Internet is suitable for you and what your criteria for success are.
One of the main attractions of the Internet is that it can reach a far wider audience than by phone, letter, conferences, exhibitions and mail-shot put together – a new worldwide market unrestricted by the usual restrictions of time, place and cost. It can be more difficult to target particular groups this way, however.

Decide on your objectives. Do you want to:

- Sign up new customers?
- Worry your competitors?
- Keep in touch with suppliers?

How will you measure success?

- Numbers of visits?
- Numbers of enquiries?
- Numbers of sign-ups/subscribers?
- Level of feedback?
- Features in the Press?

Remember that, as with all marketing efforts, gauging the contribution to the bottom line is problematic.

2. Look at what others have done
Explore WWW sites – the shop-windows – of other organisations, including any similar to your own, and see what you like and what you don't. Look closely at the style and presentation of their layout, the typeface or font style, the use of colour, graphics and icons to catch the eye, the time taken for pages to appear, especially when they include still and moving images. Ask yourself if you are sufficiently interested to go back and look again, and why? Would you tell others about it? Is there anything you would wish to emulate, adopt, modify or reject?

3. Identify an Internet Access Provider to work with.
Renting space on a computer run by an Internet Access
Provider is becoming an established method for getting onto
the WWW. You can go it alone by setting up your own
server, but this approach requires a more substantial
investment in resources, skills and knowledge. The
advantage of running your own server is the full and
immediate control you gain in updating your pages and
monitoring their usage. The disadvantage is the cost, not
merely in the hardware to cater for many simultaneous
users, but also in the technical resource needed to maintain
and develop the system. Step back to Monday for a
breakdown of the issues involved. At the moment using a
server such as that offered by increasing numbers of
providers is a cheaper, no-risk option. These companies
include BTNet, Demon, EUNet, IBM Global Networks, and
Pipex. There is also a growing number of independent Web

publishing houses. Again, refer back to Monday for a list of telephone numbers.

When selecting an Internet Access Provider bear in mind the following questions:

- What are their rates compared to those of others?
- How much are they willing to help and guide as part of their fee?
- If this help is limited, do they offer advice on constructing and designing pages on a consultancy basis?
- Do they provide regular reports on who visits your pages, when they visit, and how long they stay?
- What is their policy on updating the pages?
- Are they friendly and helpful?
- Do they use a language you can understand or is it all technobabble?
- Are they a quick, opportunistic start-up or have they been around for some time?
- Who else is using them and for which services?
- Do they have plans for introducing secure and confidential financial transactions? (Others will if they don't.)

4. Remember that the traditional requirements of innovation and creativity for quality advertising still apply.
Use a graphic designer if you can afford it, but make sure that the designer understands the medium of the Internet. Practices particularly appropriate to the content of WWW pages include:

- Making sure your branding or image remain consistent
- Giving value beyond marketing description so that customers will want to come back. For example, Holiday Inn offers direct booking for its hotels; Visa provides a search facility for the nearest cash dispenser; Federal Express offers a way to track the status of a package
- Making the pages clear, short and to the point, readable, unconfusing, free of jargon and waffle; there is a greater need for immediacy and brevity when people are paying for on-line time to look at your pages
- Keeping them up to date, new and fresh
- Avoiding too many graphics which take time to load on the screen and can be boring
- Providing imaginative links to enable customers to skip to related information instead of merely scrolling or turning pages; make it easy for people to find their way around
- Creating links to other computers such as those of collaborators, partners, suppliers, satisfied customers or related information sources; and from them to you
- Making it interactive by asking for feedback, comment and details of requirements; get customers to specify their own product preferences
- Making it expandable in the future

5. Make sure you try out your pages on a variety of browsers
Different browsers can present the same information in
different ways. Check that your pages remain as you
intended them to look, especially on Netscape and Mosaic.

*6. Remember the two forms of access: full-access and
dial-up.*
Those with a leased line can handle graphics quicker than
those with dial-up. The latter may prefer a 'text only'
version. For information on dial-up access, look back to
Monday.

What are the cost factors?

The cheapest form of advertising is to target specific
newsgroups but do use this approach with caution. It will
involve time in identifying the groups (see Tuesday), writing
suitable messages, sending them and receiving replies. The
time and cost spent in connection to the Internet is minimal.

Unless your organisation is already part of the Internet, you
will have to rent space from an Internet Access Provider in
order to market on the WWW. The cost will depend on
factors such as:

- The amount of space you buy, usually quoted in
  megabytes, but translatable into pages
- The amount of development work required on your
  information to structure it to work on the WWW
- The use of an experienced graphic designer familiar
  with the techniques needed for success on the
  Internet

- The levels of sophistication and use of graphics in design
- The numbers and types of hypertext links to other documents or sources on other computers
- The method and frequency of updating and refreshing it

At 1996 prices, a simple, straightforward 'shop-front' of a couple of pages would come perhaps to no more than a few hundred pounds. A site running to a hundred pages or more with greater sophistication and functionality including forms, various types of interactivity and clever links and connections could cost up to twenty or thirty thousand pounds to develop.

What kind of marketing strategies can be used?

If, as we have seen, brash advertising and overt aggression are to be avoided, what other kinds of marketing can be carried out on the Internet? Here are a few examples:

- Catalogues, company contacts and pricing information
- Product announcements and press releases
- Promotional notices of special sales
- Documentation and manuals
- Market research and customer surveys
- Reviews and service evaluations
- Customer service information

- Recruitment notices
- Dialogue with and involvement for the customer

Summary

What are the key criteria for success?

- Decide what you want to achieve and how to measure it
- Decide whom you wish to target
- Don't rely too much on experience of the 'paper' medium
- Decide whether or not to employ a graphic designer
- Use graphics with care
- Keep your visitors interested with something new
- Try to get them involved
- Make it easy to see what is available
- Aim for consistency of 'look' and 'feel', particularly in branding
- Ask for statistics on who is looking at which page, when and how often
- Ask for customer feedback on how comfortable they feel with your pages

Having decided to market on the Internet, the next step would be to buy and sell services. How do you pay for goods on the Internet and what other business issues are there to be aware of?

These are the subjects for Saturday.

Issues for managers

We are in a period of transition where the Internet is no longer the exclusive preserve of academics and computer nerds, but is not yet the dynamic business medium enabling full commercial transactions. That is clearly the direction, however, in which it is moving.

So as managers begin to make use of the Internet, what are the issues to be aware of? Today we will look at diverse, sometimes contentious issues which the information community worldwide is struggling to master. These concern:

- The political arena
- Technological progress
- Intellectual property and copyright
- International law
- Information overload
- Security and control
- Electronic money
- Taxation
- Costs and prices
- Running the virtual business
- Making money on the Internet

We are not suggesting that managers have an obligation to master the Internet through use of technical sources and applications. But it is increasingly important to be aware of developments and keep up to date with changes through the daily and professional press because of the issues discussed here. With commercial organisations and financial institutions putting their weight and development resources into the Internet, opportunities or threats to your business are now presenting themselves at an even faster pace than before.

The political arena

The Internet is firmly on the agenda of the European Commission, the G7 group of countries and the US Senate. Although there is no overall, coherent policy emerging for the UK, there are growing signs of disparate government initiatives. For example, the Treasury disseminates information on its activities through the WWW and there is also a CCTA UK Government information site. (See Thursday for addresses.) The DTI has kick-started efforts to examine the potential of the Internet for communications and business, and a recent government report on using the networks for education and training purposes indicates that the changing Internet might well have a vital role to play.

Key areas which governments have to address sooner or later, such as regulation and funding, are discussed later today.

Technological progress

A technological future has been described so much in the recent past as to engender cynicism. It was always just around the corner. Now it really is coming with formerly different and separate technologies converging,

particularly those of data transmission, file transfer, data
compression, encryption and the mix of text with sound,
graphics and video. Again, while these are technologies for
specialists, the implications for business can no longer be
ignored as a dream, or nightmare, of the future.

Intellectual property and copyright

As soon as any intellectual property – documents or images,
graphs or text – is available through the Internet, then it
(currently) has no monetary value as most information is
available free to all. This is changing with new controls
emerging to turn surfers into potential customers or
subscribers. But the problem goes deeper than that. If, in
due course, a customer pays for a document on the Internet,
and receives that document via the Internet, copyright law
exists to stop him or her changing its appearance and

retransmitting it, either free or for a fee to thousands of others, for example, on the open newsgroups. But copyright law is hard enough to police and enforce in the real world; on the Internet it becomes virtually impossible.

Some have said that the Internet will bring about a massive change to copyright legislation, others that copyright itself will influence the character of business on the Internet.

Although copyright can be horrendously complex, there are fundmentally two things to remember:

(i) documents you, or your organisation, have produced are yours to dispose of in any appropriate legal manner you wish

(ii) documents, or pictures, or designs – intellectual property – produced by others are not available for you to re-copy, or retransmit without permission, payment or a licence.

It is increasingly accepted that technological developments have now far outstripped the capacity of current copyright legislation to control the passage of intellectual property. This issue is currently stretching the legislative bodies of the US Senate and the EU. The focus of copyright is also shifting towards the act of transmitting a document as opposed to just copying it. In the meantime be wary of making your valuable documentation available over the net; it could rapidly lose any commercial value you attach to it.

It is not yet certain what the outcome of this will be, although one possibility is that it might well lead to experimentation with imaginative pricing policies.

When an item consists of intellectual property that can be delivered to the customer via the Internet, ease of reproduction and retransmission may initiate lower pricing for that item in order to reduce the incentive for piracy. The Internet's very character could, as business takes hold, make things cheaper than they have been through traditional means.

International law

Material available in some countries is banned in others. Cases of videos, magazines and court rulings are commonplace. Yet the Internet can now enable such material to cross international frontiers literally at the click of a button. The Internet is no respector of national borders and laws, and at the moment, controls are wholly absent.

Pornography over the Internet has been much publicised but it is not the only danger. A 'Terrorist's Handbook' containing instructions for building different types of bombs has been available for downloading from the Internet.

One solution is for the Internet to become self-regulating. Although some providers are exploring this with voluntary electronic 'tagging' of 'adult' material which could be screened out by specially configured software on the user's PC, this is resisted by the traditional free spirit lobby. In any event it could lead to a confusion of standards and expectations and encourage hackers.

Another solution is legislative regulation of the Internet. In the USA, a Telecoms Reform Bill is setting out to criminalise the sending of any material described as 'obscene, lewd, lascivious, filthy or indecent' in pioneer legislation. This would make Internet Access Providers responsible for such material passing through their lines and liable to closure.

In the UK, defamation on the Internet is seen as the next potential growth area of litigation. An attempt at new legislation to tackle libel on the Internet has resulted in the Defamation Bill which makes the individual who committed the libel responsible, rather than the Internet Access Provider.

Information overload

Problems associated with managing information, particularly too much of it, are accentuated by the Internet. Coping strategies include:

- Knowing where and how information can be obtained, rather than storing it in case a need arises
- Working out personal screening procedures, for example culling out the chaff by means of source of origin or eliminating on subject or one-line headers
- Using software for relevance ranking rather than scanning hundreds of documents
- Not overloading internal networks with garbage by passing on messages which might be of 'interest' to others
- Restricting yourself to needs and 'must haves' by asking yourself, when faced with a pile of information if you would have gone looking for it in the first place
- Thinking in terms of useable intelligence instead of useful data

- Resorting to the delete key, and making the problem disappear!

Security and control

Lack of security is a major concern and one of the factors inhibiting business from using the Internet on a wide scale. But proving that you are who you say you are is not an easy business on a network not originally designed for such a purpose.

If you have a customer who wishes to order a product at least three developments need to take place before such a transaction can take place reliably and efficiently:

- Ensuring that transactions can be private and confidential
- Authenticating the user and authorising access
- Delivering a guaranteed level of performance

We shall now look at each of these in turn.

Privacy and confidentiality
The computer industry has been looking at encryption and fire-walls for some years in order to be able to protect private, sensitive or valuable documents and guarantee their safe transmission.

Firewalls are secure electronic devices which prevent unauthorised access. Encryption is the term used for scrambling messages so that only the intended recipient can read them. While there are already a number of solutions available, it is thought that encryption codes will be made virtually 'uncrackable' in the very near future. Some form of encryption allied to authentication and authorisation processes may contribute to solving the electronic copyright problem for publishers.

Authentication and authorisation
The customer and the provider need a form of mutual authentication. At the moment the most effective way of controlling access is by username and password but there is no guarantee that these are secure against interception. There are, at the time of writing, various proposals under trial covering different levels of security and authentication.

A secure network
At the moment documents and email can go missing. It does not happen often, but it can happen. Although letters go missing and faxes do not arrive, business will demand a greater level of assurance than currently exists that a document sent via the electronic networks will arrive at its intended destination. An acceptable level of performance will probably also require notification that it has done so.

A further element undergoing high speed development is that of electronic cash.

Electronic money

With the pitfalls of theft and fraud hindering financial transactions on the Internet, there are many ongoing experiments at various stages of progress:

- Microsoft is working with Visa on a system for securing credit card payments.
- Citicorp is developing an Electronic Monetary System – electronic money for banks to issue.
- The National Westminster and Midland Banks are collaborating on 'Mondex' which loads 'e-money' onto credit card sized smart cards for use at point of sale terminals.
- First Virtual Holdings has launched a credit card system using email that lets customers use credit cards on the Internet by keeping card numbers stored in a protected computer, never passing over the Internet.
- Open Market and CyberCash enable direct interaction with existing bank and credit accounts by using an independent on-line server to handle user accounts.
- DigiCash provides cash tokens and can detect double-spending and identify the user.
- Netscape Server Galleria is a showcase of Netscape customers who have built sites using Netscape Server software. Some sites have been deployed using the secure Netscape Commerce Server. They represent the earliest examples on the Internet of how to conduct business and exchange information in a secure networked environment. These sites are indicated by a golden key icon. This is a pilot system that, according to Netscape, means that it is 'safe' to put a credit card

number into the Internet. It has been reported, however, that a French student has broken the system. The *Independent* Newspaper was told by him that he would not trust his credit card number to Netscape. Although this seems to convey a salutary message, it did take him 120 workstations to break through after eight days' work!

These experiments and others are on trial. It is predicted that consumers doing business on the Internet will in due course find that electronic money may afford greater privacy than a traditional credit card. It may also prove cheaper for banks to handle than the usual paper-based transaction.

But if your e-money is stored on a PC and the system crashes, it could be lost forever. And hackers are not going to go away. And how will counterfeiters be prevented from spreading fake e-cash?

Despite concerns such as these, experts predict that
solutions, if not standards, are not far away.

Taxation

There are probably hundreds of millions of dollars' worth of
work crossing national borders each year without payment
of customs or duties. How will tax be paid and collected on
future transactions? Tracking and controlling reportable
income pose problems of enormous magnitude in a cashless
society where technological capability has once again
outstripped the ability of the regulators to control it. The
move towards self-assessment in the UK seems in tune with
the argument for self-regulation, but the key to the process
is still based on the ability of the authorities to initiate audits
and checks. At the time of writing, inland revenue
authorities are struggling with the issue of tax control and
regulation on the Internet.

Costs and prices

Why is document transmission on the Internet so cheap?
Will prices stay so low? Data packets – information coded
by your PC into binary 0s and 1s – are much cheaper than
voice signals because a telecom line can carry a lot of them
at the same time thus sharing the cost between different
users. The line can carry only one voice signal at a time. The
latter makes accounting and billing easier. The former
makes it a nightmare – one reason for a cheap flat rate.
Several factors may alter this in the future, notwithstanding
the costs of introducing ISDN, or fibre optics:

- As traffic on the Internet increases and one form of communication perhaps takes primacy over another, the telecommunications companies may simply change their pricing structure
- Depending on how the Internet is financed in the future – by government, private enterprise or users – pricing may change

Running the virtual business

Once you are up on the Internet you cannot sit back and wait for the results, far from it, it's just the beginning. Updating your site is important but so is keeping up to date with developments. Keeping abreast of changes, advances and new experiments is all the more vital as obsolescence takes on a new meaning on the Internet.

Doing business on the Internet will provide a new scale of opportunity for customer focus and customer care. Increased two-way communication needs resourcing, so will responding to a new type of informed and demanding consumer, called the 'prosumer' some years ago by Alvin Toffler in his book *The Third Wave.*

One of the major impacts of electronic networking will be on the way we work, and whence we do it. If most, if not all, business communications and transactions become both practical and effective on a secure Internet, then there is less need to be tied to the desk, the office or the workplace at all.

Teleworking is already a reality for thousands of people.
Without the need for a place of work, how will the business

be structured? The impact on organisations and individuals
may be considerable. One implication is that short- or fixed-
term contracts, already on the increase, will become the
norm. People will sell their skills to fit project and personal
needs. The implications for meeting workers' social needs
are also far-reaching; already people have their meetings
through video and tele-conferences in cyberspace. How will
companies carry out the essential functions they do today?
Will some functions become obsolete, or merely change and
adapt to fit the new working environment?

Making money on the Internet

We saw earlier in the week how some companies are using
imagination and innovation to add value for their customers.
Some companies have already gone a step further and have
started to make a profit out of Internet business.

In early 1995, there were many examples of all kinds of businesses exploring the potential of the Internet, but it was difficult to trace any reported examples of successful entrepreneurship and revenue generation amid all the euphoria of press hype and speculation. By mid-1995, however, examples had begun to appear.

Netscape, with its WWW browser, was floated on the US Stock Exchange and became worth $1bn in six months. It will be interesting to see how Netscape shapes up against Microsoft's Windows '95 which will offer its own browser. According to the publicity, Microsoft Network requires you only to click on one button and have your credit card ready. It promises easy access to messaging, shopping and a wide range of companies providing information and services for everyone.

Firefox, a Midlands, UK-based company, sells software which provides a filter to screen off parts of the Internet which companies do not want their employees to access. Internet Access Providers are into clear profit once their subscriptions have covered the cost of their hardware.

This phase involves 'Internet-related' products and services. The next phase involves 'information content providers' such as advertising agencies, games providers, newspapers, financial data services, bookshops and publishers which are, by the very nature of their products and services, more easily adapted to electronic provision and delivery. The third phase will include those businesses which are not necessarily 'Internet-related', but which have recognised the opportunities of buying and selling on the WWW.

Conclusion

The Internet has made, and will continue to make, enormous inroads into our personal and working lives. Today we have indicated some areas of consideration for the immediate future and raised questions the answers to which will have a determining influence on the progress of the Internet.

How soon will it be before:

- Most large companies aggressively encourage telecommuting?
- Modems are commonplace in the home?
- Pricing strategies for communications are modified?
- Standards for security and secure payment are in place?
- Hacking and viruses pose less of a threat?
- A government policy emerges?
- Better quality information outweighs dross on the Internet?
- Business can be guaranteed the levels of performance to run the virtual business?
- The high-speed, high-performance and high-capacity telecommunications cables – the much hyped broadband cables capable of piping 500 channels to the home – are installed?

Some of these questions will be answered sooner rather than later. In the meantime it is important to be aware of the issues for you and your business, and, if you haven't yet, to take some action.

The organisation, however large or small, public or private, profit-making or charitable, manufacturing or service, needs to know how rapidly the Internet is changing to cater for business needs and the major issues to consider when becoming connected. It will need to establish strategies and tactics on the Internet; it will need to know which major operations need to be performed and the best way of performing them; and it will need to know how to resource them and assimilate a different scale of costs and new cost structures. Most importantly it will need to adopt a new vision, or way of looking at how the business can work without the traditional constraints of time, space or physical resources.

As a final word, put the Internet to use; many have found it rewarding and useful.

- Establish an effective connection to the Internet and promote its use within the organisation.
- Start to use email and sign up with one or two specialist discussion groups.
- Make time to explore the resources relevant to your own and the organisation's needs.
- Become familiar with the Internet so that it becomes an integrated part of your day.
- Plan to start doing business on the Internet.